Die

Poor,

Live

Forever

icon303

Die Poor, Live Forever

Die Poor, Live Forever

Dedicated to:

The Beast

Die Poor, Live Forever

Published by Coyote Blood Press
& Paradisiac Publishing.

Cover Art by icon303

ISBN: 9798713803155

IG: @icon303
Twitter: @yugo_icon303

www.icon303.com

Die

Poor,

Live

Forever

icon303

NW 21st Ave
Oakland Park, FL

Upon arrival in South Florida, Yugo and the Beast landed with some close friends. His stay there was foreshadowed by the agreement he could be there a week and then he had to find his own place.

Being a man of his word, Yugo found a room for rent in a bad neighborhood from a gay Israeli man, Aziz. He had served in the Israeli army, but now waits tables in a Mexican restaurant. The man had two asshole dogs and a cat, so the Beast had to stay in the small room most of the time Yugo was at work.

The day Yugo had moved in, a Peruvian man fresh out of a Peruvian prison, was moving out and a younger, Latin woman, with three kids, was overdosing in her doorway. Yugo would never leave his 7x10 room unless he had to go to work.

Aziz went to NYC for Thanksgiving to see family for a week. The first few nights he was gone, a crackhead broke in and trashed the apartment, screaming about circuit boards that they couldn't find. When Aziz returned from New York, he began asking Yugo for more money than the agreement they had already signed. Yugo resisted and Aziz promptly told him to leave and called the police. Having had that happen more times in his life than one would like, Yugo ran to his room, threw clothes in a bag, grabbed his bowl, weed, and the Beast, and left the house with the man yelling and threatening fading into the distance.

While they were walking Yugo stopped next to a couch on its back at the curb to act like he was tying his shoelaces. He stashed his pipe and weed in the bottom of the couch and continued walking hoping that the Broward County Sheriffs didn't catch up with him.

As he was walking there was a homeless man painting near a bus stop. The man stood out to

Yugo, he felt like he understood him instantly upon seeing him. Even with all the bad happening around him, Yugo never once thought of running back to the life he had before in Madlands, NY. It was at that moment when he saw the homeless artist that it finally made sense to Yugo. If Yugo had to lose everything again and again, it didn't matter. If the world rejected his mind's work, it didn't matter. Yugo was on the exact journey he wanted to be on, to create, write, and spread love, even if that means dying in the gutter.

The Beast has been Yugo's last foot in reality ever since they met in the back of a pig farm. Even while his psychedelic boundaries are being taunted, she was the only soul to love him anyways. She has seen the highs and the lows, staying next to Yugo through death-defying stints of poverty and homelessness. Together they've saved each other's lives and helped one another grow, rebuild, and heal through depression, loss, and relocation to see a better life.

Yugo expects nothing more than to pass on a park bench, like so many other great artists and writers before him, and he's completely ok with it. Yugo could care less about material belongings or financial stability, as it has never made him feel fulfilled. The only things that have never left him were his Beast and his creativity. In his eyes, art and poetry are the only way he'll live forever.

Die Poor, Live Forever is the journey of Yugo Levchenko and his Beast post-Two Years. A thorough compilation of poetry from his day-to-day life in South Florida depicting his realization that he may have to die poor for this love of art and humanity to live on forever; an exploratory delve into his psyche, past, present, future, morals and beliefs.

"

The first requisite

for immortality

is death.

"

- Stanisław Jerzy Lec

Floating Coconuts Part 1

Make the dream, make the dream

It just takes a bit of kelp

And floating coconuts

A standing bench, a standing bench

Makes the old days seem farther

Like floating coconuts

An old man, an old man

Only had a bag of food

And floating coconuts

Closed umbrellas, closed umbrellas

Let the husk get soaked

Like floating coconuts

Dreams to fruition, dreams to fruition

The man throws away his bag and left

The floating coconuts

Windowsill Bathroom

They called and said
They had a job,
"I think we have a lizard problem
In the bathroom."

I said,
"Yeah. I could use
The money."

"Good. Get all the shit
Off of the ledge
And meet us in the office."

"Fuck this."

Propaganda #930

There's a certain level of pain
That becomes apparent in any language.

Pranksters and Politicians

Hunter would be happy to know
Heathens like us carry on
What he and Kesey started.

It's always been easy
To turn a friend into an enemy
After the friend-watch hits zero.

I'm going to try not to this time.

Moral vs. Monetary

Eating steak and eggs
With the same view as normal,
Just with more plumes
Of smoke rising
From the city ahead.

Eating some oatmeal,
Hoping we can
Just use Clorox Wipes
On the chicken bourgeoisie
And be done with it.

Don't worry, sweetheart.
We have contingencies in place
To keep us warm until
The sun decides it is time
To come back up again.

I know it is cold out, baby,

But they can't hold us for long.

We have the grit of growing up

Without things like

Protection and stability.

We were all real

Before the flashes came.

Nothing but boom claps

And threaded choices;

Dotted with wrong decisions

On either side of the

Correct sewn path.

Its only strength coming from

The dual and doubled

Choices from either side

Of the caste spectrum.

Help us now.

Propaganda #356

If you skip out on this fight,

Then skip out of all the fights.

We don't need you.

If you come to this fight,

Then go to the next

And the next and the next

And let's move down together

And ram it home to

Any opposition like

A fucking train;

It's a zealot's world outside.

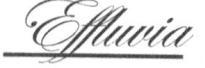

Lose all the fake.

The friend in your face

With a dagger in hand.

The unreasonable.

Realize when you leave

This plane of existence,

You take away with you,

And wear,

The memory of every face

You spit in.

Bad Salad

Cramped like a bad salad;

Random coughs slaughtered the peace

And 17 languages conversed alone.

The line to slaughter was long,

But timid.

2 hours, 2 hours.

The only positive object

Was the roof blocking us all

From being wet cattle.

S113 is being served at station number 3

And I need to move my feet

For the next at the chopping block.

Just breathe, 2 hours.

Stare at the brightest shirt

And pray your number is next.

R187 is being served at number 15.

2 hours, did I miss it?

I didn't miss the ass in yoga pants

At number 10.

2 hours, D135 served at number 20.

2 hours until he coughs again

Right next to a pink ribbon

He wouldn't let sit next to him.

Someone could've saved us.

Maybe the lady talking on two phones

At once could ask someone for help,

We needed it 2 hours ago.

They're two numbers away from mine

And it might still take 2 hours.

Here we go, about time.

Hi, how are you?

I'd be better if I

Wasn't here the 2 hours prior

To the 2 hours before that.

I think in 2 hours I'll be

High enough I won't even

Remember the past day,

Let alone 2 hours.

Propaganda #547

Did we learn nothing

From Rome?

The paradigm is that

When you call for justice under freedom,

Then you must also try to justify the injustices;

There will always be a tug of war.

If those for justice are free,

So are those for injustice.

And if you can't handle

The migraine of the

Proceeding ignorance,

You're a fascist and communist.

If all of those are thwarted,

Well, damn it, we'll in-fight.

Pick a side, you bastard!

Are you left, or right?!

Like a man with two dicks,

I dress to both.

I dress for none of the above

And all of the below.

The only way to win a fixed game

Is to not play.

The only way to win

Is to lose.

Wonderland Ranch

Behind that row of trees,

Behind that field of grains,

A ranch waits for the one.

A beauty that turned eerie,

With its happiness feigned,

Another stranger was shunned.

Oh, this house, this house;

Guarded by trees and peril,

And still wounded with squatters,

It still seemed to shine from inside.

An overgrown bioluminescence

Given to all things that find it hard to live.

Large, stained, white shutters

Outlined hidden hazels deep within,

And a rocky foundation that crumbled to stability,

Brought a scourge of abuse for years.

Resilience in chaotic turpitude
Can usually be found in those who never felt love.

A step through the front door
Wouldn't even bring closure.
No starting anew on an adjoining wall;
The house wants an occupant
To feed the fireplace that's built already.
The pictures and stories watch it all happen.

Some fallen timber only accents the vines,
Turning the wind into a whistle;
Calling all things wild and unsheltered.
No wonder everything 8-legged
Takes solace in your abandon,
It can be quite alluring.

As bridged as it may be,
No good was gained
When amity won.

The tide pools on this beach,

Are landlocked and tamed;

Missing your fun.

Cheers to the safety you represent.

Think.

A Rebel's Last Wish

Write like no one is reading,

Like your message they'll never hear;

Because they never will.

Yet, we are immortal through our writing.

The government smells like chemicals

And it burns my esophagus.

This must be modern day biological warfare,

Pretty poison mixed in aluminum.

Load me up, load me up.

I'm the ghost of Tom Joad's

Self-immolation in your cerebellum.

The bidet in the back of your mind

That tells you belligerence is necessary.

The wick you thought burned out

As you went to pick up the dynamite.

Who else would dare interrupt

Your regularly scheduled programming?

Me.

icon303.

Read.

Write.

Speak.

Propaganda #875

If you want to study history,
Look no further than ourselves,
For it isn't long before we are.

Idleness

All the good
Little hooligans were down
At the local watering hole
Indulging in one of the worst drugs
Known to man and womankind alike;
Next to nicotine, that is.

These poor little imps
Sing woes from the first world
And most will never
Have to clean up
The brains of their heroes.

But, what can I judge?
I've abused them all in copious amounts
And haven't regretted a single bit.

There were times we needed
To know the ATM fees

At different locations
To juggle the balance but still never went
To sleep on the ground again.

But Still, I Said Goodbye

Just the first time

I saw you is all

It's easy to fall

It's easy to fall

Looking back it was

Harder on the ledge

Throughout it all

Throughout it all

I will balance any edge

As long as

It has

You

Propaganda #001

Fuck the boundaries.

The black or white,

Conservative or liberal;

Poor or rich,

Male or female.

First and foremost, we are humans.

Everything outside of that

Is a construct; a fugazi mote to our lives.

And as humans we have a

Tribal need for inclusion.

We make up imaginary belongings

To encompass ourselves in our beliefs

And negate the outside world.

That's the issue with inclusion...

The flipside is

Equally as powerful and excludes

Everything outside your reality.

There's a huge difference
Between inclusion and acceptance.
It's the difference
Between knowledge and wisdom,
Words and action.

The only boundaries that are
Worth commiserating are:
Good and bad,
Intellect and ignorance.
A beautiful day
Starts the moment
That realization comes.

Madlands, NY

The changing of
Leaves beckons this
Eerily familiar feeling.

The beautiful sights covered with
Indisposed people.

You're either born resilient
Or destined to comply.

And I,
I will never dream of
Anything less than leaving.

Many reasons I'd be crazy to trust again,
Where even the dumbest think they're clever
With no conscious.

In this town, this town.

Losing Little Ones

I witnessed today
A little boy and girl,
Eyes bright with excitement,
Cheering, "Daddy!"
As I walked through the door
And I cried.

To have that
Would make me feel
Like the wealthiest man
In any universe.

To have what I never did.

Well... to have
What I never got to keep.

Her birthday is soon,
On April 24th.

I was only 19.

12 long years ago.

Almost a different life.

A different world,

Running heroin from Harlem.

I was outside a Burger King,

Down the street from the Apollo,

Thinking about that

Cute blonde hair.

I came back in the snow

And took a bus to see you.

Your mother bought

Jelly filled doughnuts

And we laughed eating breakfast.

I watched you mimic

All my mannerisms,

And steal your mom's hat

To wear backwards like me

And my heart with it.

A Barbie Lego kingdom
That you needed protected
By Ninja Turtles.

I cried when I left your room.

And even harder
When I left your life.

I hope one day
You can see
I did it
For you
And not
For
Me.

I'm sorry.

Propaganda #731

The terrible tragedy

Of the Japanese people

Is that their intelligence

Has always been limited

To having to answer to,

And ask permission from,

An authority

That only cared about

Its own lineage.

Disguise

Coronavirus is

The new mono.

Kiss me baby.

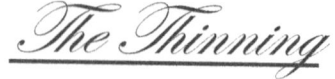

The Thinning

Having a picture of Amy Winehouse
In your bar is like:

Putting a picture of Biggie and Tupac
On bullets.
It's like putting a picture of Kobe
On the side of a helicopter.
Like putting a picture of Mac Miller
On fentanyl and coke baggies,
Like giving kids shirts
With Epstein's face.

I need you to think more.

Propaganda #641

Has nobody realized
The "Get Out of Jail Free" card
In monopoly
Is white privilege?

You Better Say Your Prayers Before Bed

And if I die before I wake
I pray my word the masses take
And mend a time as large as ours;
Spark the mind who'll take it far.

Let the words from my mind
Manifest into the bullet to load the gun
And give it to Princip to change the time.
I suspect Ferdinand was loathed for fun.

A sick prank to laugh about later,
Redrawing every line but the equator.

To Whom It May Concern:

I just want to fuck you

One last time.

Propaganda #951

Feelings are nothing more

Than the window

Of which our soul peers.

The filters for the

Camera of our brain.

A never-ending sepia,

Or a cold light blue,

A dancing red or sedating purple.

Emotions are nothing to be feared,

But rather acknowledgeable sentients

From deep within

That see all.

That recorded every time you fell

Or every time you cried and

Reminds you not to do those again.

Laughs with you

In an emerald green vignette
And encourages you to do more.
Reminds you how warm and safe
It is inside another's arms...

Feelings aren't
The people who
Took advantage of them.

7-3-8

The moon would be beautiful, yeah?

Peace and quiet;

The only desire is sunlight and oxygen.

You can keep yourself

And how you treat each other

Back on that rock of selfishness.

Maybe there I wouldn't

Grimace at the neighbors

And stay to myself.

How beautiful.

Floating Coconuts Part 2

I've always felt
A connection to the stars,
Especially learning a dog
Followed Orion.

Something about having
The Beast next to me
Makes it all make sense.

The coconuts looked
Like part of the cosmos,
Hanging there…
Almost like they belonged.

Hard to believe a 10 lbs. fruit
Is suspended in midair
Until you get as high as I do.

Propaganda #101

When life is bleak

It's like you lose

All the knowledge you gained

Along with the fun.

Farewell to the Man

Dear Feather and Jim,

Everything has a cycle. Nathaniel Hawthorne
Encompassed it well with his quote:
"Families are always rising and falling in America."
Some cycles are long and never-ending;
Some are short with a saddened farewell.

During Yugo's run with The Ledger,
And Fatehouse Media,
Which has been an endearing experience
That will be remembered,
He has met some amazing people.

Feather-
For all the bothersome shenanigans
You put up with, I thank you.
You gave me the space to be me
And *that* means more to me

Than you will ever know.

You graced each of the employees' days

With smiles, motivation, determination,

And a feeling of belonging.

I couldn't have asked for a better manager, leader, or

Entertainer.

Jim-

I thank you for also putting up with my craziness.

From the kidnapping of the food in the refrigerator,

To the requests for a Segway and rubber band guns,

You have been the epitome of cool.

James Dean himself would get out a notepad.

I thank you a million times

For giving a kid like me

All of the acceptance I could've asked for.

It's with a deep heart

That I regretfully inform you

That my last day of employment

Will be Nov. 1st, 2017.

This area has been quite unfriendly to me

Over the course of my life

And I appreciate you guys giving me

At least one happy place to remember.

Thank you for your understanding

And everything you've done for me.

Words could never describe how appreciative I am.

Yugo "icon303" Levchenko

The stars are shining
So bright tonight.

It's like they're shining for us
Almost 7 years later to the day;
15, if you count high school
And all the hell with it.

I know you hate me,
But I'll always dream
Of the night I first held
Your shaking hands.

Propaganda #412

Challenge your past.

Challenge history.

Challenge your elders.

Declaration of Defiance
Towards the Empire-istic Shadow

We,

The People of the Revolution of the Tired Company,

Led by the valiant and self-less Yugo Levchenko,

Declare acts of defiance against the oppressive

And un-just drafting of colleagues into the ranks of

Stormtroopers.

The acts of defiance will include,

But are not limited to:

Pranks,

Posting of pranks on various social media sites,

Sleep-ins,

Direct opposition to rules and regulations,

Purposeful sabotage of superiors' lunch time,

Pillow/water balloon/rubber band fights,

And a severe lack of personal hygiene

By those participating.

It is not moral,

Nor gracious,

To draft such young, innocent lives

Into the monstrous and mind-numbing

Manipulation of thoughts

By the actions of the long shadow

Of the outstretched hand

That is Fatehouse Media's expectations of conduct.

How can one expect one to be so uniform

When they, themselves,

Are meandering outside the lines

In the coloring book called morals?

Case in point, Feather Hulk.

Feather was once a person

Born of two parents and possibly has siblings.

She had a pulse and a voice of her own;

She would even care about helpless animals

From time to time.

One could even state her as having a heart.

Mrs. Hulk was drafted into The Shadow

And currently goes by the pseudonym "*FTR-347*"

And no longer associates with us lowly rebels.

Until she is returned to us

As she once was,

We will not rest.

We will keep a candle lit until

That outstretched hand contracts

Into a fist from anger.

Furthermore,

The Revolution demands

An office wide "Pajama Day"

In remembrance of Feather Hulk,

Whether or not we get her back.

This is not a request. Rather, a demand

Payable through comfortability

For the inconvenience of losing a loved one.

As powerful as the Empire can be, I must remind you

Of the loss in productivity and concentration

That a simple mohawk and kilt can cause.

It may seem like a mountain won't crumple

Until the right pebble is strewn.

Sincerely,

Yugo Levchenko and the REM Revolution of the

Tired Company

"If a law is unjust, a man is not only right to disobey it,

he is obligated to do so."

-Thomas Jefferson

Routes Home

An ambulance at the church
With her friends praying,

She'll make it through.
Little do they know
She's being praying for this
Longer than she's known
Any of the collection plate patrons.

Was *God* answering her or them?
Saying goodbye, don't look!
I have to give you some Risperidone.
As soon as it kicks in,
We'll just go for a little drive.

Don't stay hunched for too long,
You have to enjoy new friends and
The change of pace in your new home.

I won't forget the Alvin's
Jenga block home.

Icons Before Me

I need Che to remind me
"The true revolutionary
Is guided by a great
Feeling of love,"

And

Where is the poster of
Mevlüt Mert Altıntaş
Standing over his oppressor
In the commercial for freedom?

We need a reminder,
There is an emptiness.
Where are they now?

Can we bring back Assata
And praise at her pedestal?
A flower for every day

In isolation for us.

Take me to Oscar Zeta Acosta,

Wherever he is, to roam

With bountiful brown buffalo

And every single person that's Gonzo'd.

I want to get drunk with Bukowski

Off the rum we just ran with Capone.

I want to smoke a cigar with Luciano

While we talk asylum with Snowden.

Trip with Thompson, Ginsberg, and Kerouac,

Hitching rides from Black Panthers.

Give me a day to get blazed with Rick Simpson

And debate universal truths with Einstein.

I want to share a cell with Mandela

And invent adventures with Hofmann.

I want to play football with Bob
And network with Buynak.

Take me to Tesla's dimension
With electromagnetic fields
To protect our futures
In parallel times.

Can you give us back Hughes
To slick back the hatred
That has festered ever since
We lost him?

We need a reminder
There is another way.
Where are they now?

Where is Sagan's last book
So we can indulge in his knowledge
Before we tuck our kids in bed
And drift into the stars

And

Bonnie Parker's car
To escape the authorities
Persecuting the freethinkers
Like me?

Sincerely,
icon303

Propaganda #620

It's sort of sad
And beautiful at the same time
That we have to balance
Our checkbooks with
Food on one plank
And bullets on the other.

Polish for Your Dollar

Another dull moment
And I swear
I'm going to fuckin'
Capsize this dinge-hole.

Fuckin' snowbirds
And spring breakers
Are rolling in COVID-19.

Flights are half off and
Cruises are cancelled
From here on out.

Verona Rigsby

Looking for caretakers
And purposeful mischief.
Strange names are accepted.

Must be why I woke up
To 200 friend requests
On Facebook this afternoon.

Those caretakers came to care
And they brought with them
All their strange names.

Mischief tactfully lagged behind,
Maybe only a week out
From landing in Normandy.

A lady on a hill watched
And sang through it all until
We wept from overindulgence.

She waved back and turned,
Probably to return to the boom
And intricacies of evermore.

Must be why I woke up
Face-first on the tiles,
Late to another arrangement.

Forgive me and love me
Regardless the universe I'm from,
I never had a caretaker before.

That's why I'm looking,
Can't you see that?
I'm not aloof.

I just need some saltwater
In my daily diet
To combat the fresh air.

Propaganda #787

I've never seen such a case in
Presidential history where an
Individual's choice in a candidate
Hi-lights their level of
Intellectual ineptitude.

Mykonos Berry

I was a lot more beautiful
With you around.
Maybe not so much physically,
But how you made me feel.
I'd give it all to
Feel handsome again,
To love the most beautiful girl
I've ever met again.
It's like each one
Of the tears I caused
Lived to be ghosts
That keep me awake
And haunt the dark.
You were the prettiest
Bridge I ever burnt,
I can still smell the smoke.

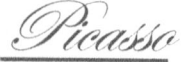

It is only once we lose everything

That we're free to do anything.

Interesting to ponder

The exact sequence

Of events that dripped us

On the canvas

And dried us in place.

The blending of

Colors that dance

To spectating eyes,

Pulling the gravity of

Attention from elsewhere

To the epicenter

Of our former selves.

The Picasso'd splatter

Of shapes and sizes

Beautifully puzzled together

And ready for unveiling.

Most people will never get to

Live their dream as they

Get to distracted

With their nose.

Propaganda #411

My great aunt

Passed away today.

I'm not even mad.

At 107,

You can do

What you want.

The Beast

Even dogs will have a day,

And some dogs have had a week.

I've had a year

That's been tough to complete.

I'd be gone if it

Weren't for you.

My biggest fear is losing you

Before it's time to part.

I wish we could've met

From the very start.

I'd gone through more

If I'd had you.

And, now you'll

Live

Forever.

Singing Swans

There will be a minuscule instance
When there is but one man left.
One lonely human alone with their *God*.
One small second, before it passes,
When they can have a conversation.

Will *God* apologize when humanity
Is but a speck of universal history?
What will they say to each other in those
Fleeting moments when life
And spirituality meet and cease?

It will obviously be too late to start over...

But what excuses will man spew
To plead for a second chance,
And will they be heard?
I believe there will be silence.
Silence will answer all,

For we're the sheep and
Jesus came with the wolves
And not with the people
Who need him most.

Because, fuck us, right?

Propaganda #290

Having money

Is like having

A big dick:

Everyone thinks

It sounds great

Until you realize

How lonely it is

When only

A small fraction

Of people can

Take it and

Enjoy it.

Outbreak day 31

It is guarded around here;
We don't go outside without
A gun in each of our waistbands.
160 cases thus far and climbing.

I'm not so worried about
The outcome(s), as we planned
For each possibility and where
We were going to go first,
Second, and third.
First: Lowes for a respirator,
Dog food, and a few day's essentials.
Second: a small gun store
To stockpile ammo and weapons.
Third: to find my daughter.

We're starting to repeat ourselves.
The weather is overcast
And forecast not promising.

But we have bullets.

So, there's that.

Lameweight

I land on
Every landing-strip
With my tongue out.
I want to be
The first person
To do acid in space.

Don't you dare
Try to stop me.
There's no room
Between zero
And one hundred
If you don't let
It exist.

I can feel
Your cold eyes
And it assures me
You don't think

I'm going to be ok.
But rest easy,

Nothing weak
Can kill such
A hardened loon.
Especially if he is
Mad at the whole
World around him.

Propaganda #516

We all need to shed

Something a bit deeper than flesh;

Damn whoever doesn't.

If you ever miss me

Just pick me up and read me

Because each cover contains

My tattered pieces within.

Fingers to the Winds

A chill came through the air
That reminded me of home and
Made an eerily familiar chill go
Down my spine, this time it

Wasn't from the acid. This time
It was for remembering the first
Fights on park avenue, the law
Stealing my car for revenue (the

Cop being someone I've known my
Whole life), the place I thought
I found my wife and the
Place I almost killed myself in

Spite of her. We're a cursed
People where I'm from. The hometown
Was a breeding ground for heretical
Vermiculite; a primordial ooze that spawns

The fungi of humanity backed by

Manifest destiny from *God* himself.

We'll need *God* to help us

If we ever want to survive

It. Dump the breaks, you won't

Need them. You stop, you die.

Live.

8 Hours Less

Could you really ever love
Someone like me? I know
We're both laying here
Next to our dogs right now,
Watching movies that remind us
Of blanket forts. I know we're both
Aching for someone to love us
The way we love them.

So, what's stopping you?
I could love you better
Than most, I'm just not as outgoing
And bear too many scars from past lives.
But a gun isn't a gun without bullets.
Almost like a house fly buzzing
In an ashtray, but only I realized
It was still alive; immortalizing yourself.

Sometimes I push myself too far

And I can't sleep because

I've died in my own dreams

A thousand times. Who would

Rather live 8 hours

Less?

Propaganda #544

Jedi always find each other.

Wouldn't it be great
If we could all live
In limbo forever?

I'll see you there.

C'est La Vie

There was a branch that swayed despite the winds
Blessing every day
That I'd watch amongst the irrationality behind my
Back at the window.

She danced and jived and put up a fight and didn't give
A damn what you said.
It's like she could see what's happening inside and
Counted every blow.

I couldn't help but wonder in-between skirmishes if
She was dancing for me.

She spelled *hope* in the sky with her finger and pushed
Me to make another day.
And, with every twist, her presence lingered as she
Danced the night away.

I went back after acquiring freedom to see if the tree

Wasn't stone.

Low and behold, my branch was holding her own.

Although there were no more leaves, she never lost the

Crook.

Never stopped her dance, even if no one looked.

I wish I could give her the hope that she gave me...

Maybe I can on a day with both of us free.

Propaganda # 246

It's easier to call yourself

A piece of shit

Than to say you love yourself

Despite the piece of shit

Things you've done.

Floating Coconuts Part 3

Am I bothered

By insults to my intelligence

Because I'm really

Innately stupid?

I think so.

Well, here I am...

The ugly and strange version

Of your adult teens;

31 at a restaurant where

Bartenders go to die.

Maybe one day

I'll walk under

A floating coconut

In the same

Position

As

Me.

Propaganda #355

It's peculiar…

China was a cunt hair away

From full-blown

Civil war

Until a pandemic

Was released.

Palliative

They always assumed she'd stay,
But she's been going to appointments
That she made years prior

Like she preplanned giving up the past
To live in the endless present.

"This is my mother?" They both asked
At a picture of a day on a frozen pond,
"And who was that skating?"

She shakily lit another cigarette
And set it next to the ones she forgot.

Inciter

Respect no authority,

Freedom is a dying ideal.

Most countries limit this,

Ours is no exception.

But who else gets discussed

In history books?

Who else do we idolize?

Sweat collected on my Glock

Tucked in my waistband

While I walked to catch my check.

Darwin already warned us

The ignorant will reproduce.

Money is for the narcissists,

Not dreamers.

Dreamers are the rebels.

And rebels have no choice

But to be fucking legends.

Because, in the end of it all,

We're just transients of mad times;

Brought together by rape and murder

And all things that rhyme with tragedy.

Die poor,

Live forever.

Propaganda #035

Most people want a place,

A purpose.

But if everyone had their calling,

There would be no one

To fill in the voids.

I love the void.

It makes me

Richer than everyone,

As I have everything

They will never know.

Let Me Turn off the Light

Tonight was the first I really saw you beam,
Sashaying across the driveway
With only a dull streetlamp to illuminate the hood
Behind you.

The flowers on your dress being the only thing to
Decorate the deterioration.
Again, it felt like the world was at peace.

I couldn't help but ravish you
No matter who was walking past.
With my hands all over you
Instinct took over.

While we watched the same scene in bliss
The rain fell and so did I.
And you'd never know that when you turn around
And kiss me before you leave it renders me paralyzed.

I count each of your steps as you walk away and

Worship the ground you just stepped on.

But you'd never know

Because I'm always behind you…

Chasing.

F. M. Esfandiari

I'm no Egyptian Pharaoh
Because I figured out how to never die.

Immortality comes from
Only dying once in life
And moving your soul
Into the minds of the amassed;
Living on in reforms
And being the scapegoat
For why we've changed.

A catalyst of
An unforeseen good.

I Do Declare...

I will never

Be a cuckold to the courts

And thank a judge

That's ready to impose

A tyrant's sentence upon me.

Propaganda #612

We waste our love

Before we understand

What we're giving

And give it to people

Who can't appreciate

Its value.

Work Wife

I came just to see you
Go ahead, pour your ills
In my glass.
Leave room for the head.

I look forward to
Our next shift.

Stand in front of
Your art exhibit
And make it shine
Just a little more.

Tell your boyfriend
I asked how he was.

Come back
And show me those pictures
You made me

Follow your Instagram

For.

It's just a matter

Of time.

Ballad of Mojo Sampson

What do you say?

Let's have another beer

And get me out

Of this doublewide.

Let's cruise a backroad

And call some girls.

Let's smoke this joint and

Down a Milwaukee before we go.

Let's laugh and forget this is

The last time we will laugh together.

What do you say?

Let's have another beer

When I get

To South Carolina

And we can drink

In the sand.

And if they run out,

We can run from our pasts

Further south to the Keys

Where the dress code is bikini only.

What do you say?

Let's have another beer

Because I'm not drunk yet,

You asshole!

I just haven't heard from you

In a while.

I find it hard to believe

You aren't home

So, wake up, wake up,

And answer the door.

I've got a plan,

What do you say?

Let's have another beer.

Propaganda #152

I said before
That time is only relevant
To our lifespans.

And, if you follow
Any sort of
Quantum physics theories
You'll realize in a
Parallel universe
You're already dead.

So, there is no more
Time left to live.

Living to Be

You'd have to be crazy to date me.
I'll get black out drunk
And run from you on a back road
When I'm supposed to meet your family.

I've been known to come home
With blood on my shirt and shoes
Ask you to throw them away
While I wash an excuse alone.

I take acid and show up tripping,
Do coke and walk around with guns.
A whiskey sipping artist that's been
Smoking DMT and candy flipping.

People have told legends for centuries
About how Coyote Blood can
And will kill you, but who listens?
Martyrs we are in those stories.

You wouldn't have survived.
Silence is where
The murder grows.

Orwell's Wet Dream

Poetry has become

The last frontier of

Freedom

I can sit here

And type all day

About how babies dying

Is mere Darwinism

And no one

Will bat an eye

Or transform a shooting

Into a floral metaphor

And no one

Would know the difference

Write

Poetry is the lens
Through which we express
How the world

Looks to those
With emotional scars

And a true study
Of their inner most
Hidden thoughts

That are never shown

A look at those who
Hurt and those who
Do the hurting

Like X-ray vision

To our hearts

Read

Propaganda #906

My money is

In the bank

So, I can finally

Stop wearing socks.

Don't peacock me

Because my plumage

Is prettier.

On the Beach

You want your money?

I'm trying...
I quit my previous job
Because we were
Supposed to be open
The 2nd of February.

Here it is,
Almost March,
And not only haven't
We been not open,
But I haven't been paid.

I turned down
Other jobs
That I could've started
Making money at
A month ago.

But the beach was nice
And so were the girls.
Nothing better than
Seeing beauty all around
While getting fucked

On the beach.

Fuck the money,
I'll take the coitus.

Clifftop Views

Yugo always knew,

If life didn't kill him before hand,

That he'd end up

On the edge a cliff by thirty.

Listening to the gravel

Fall into limbo beneath his feet

Made the feeling of *Déjà Vu*

All the more

Surreal and intimidating.

Propaganda #421

How are we

The *United* States

When all we focus on

Are things that divide us?

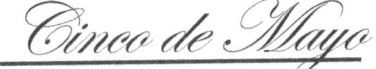 Cinco de Mayo

Each shade of
Blue and green
Deepened my appreciation
For nature.

Watching the Beast flit about
So full in such a
Fleeting moment froze time.

Each grain of sand
Stuck to my leg
Took a piece of me
With it back into the ocean.

The zipping of bees
Made room for more flowers,
Even when there isn't any.

Swells crashed to shore

And cured the stress of the day.

I made little holes
With my feet in the sand
To watch them wash away,
Much like the stress of the year.

I'd once say, "Like snow on
A hot tin roof."
But thankfully,
I'll never have to
See snow again.

Tired from the 2-mile hike,
The Beast slowed to a lay.
She bit at the waves and
Lazily taught me the way
To find peace in the past.

I bet she never imagined,
Shivering on plywood,
That there was ever even

Such a thing as the beach.

Our paws bled for a week,
But all was worth it;
Nothing a little Aloe Vera
Can't fix.

It's not like it didn't take
A bit of pain to end up here
To begin with.
I think we can deal.

Sunday is for Church

Today was interrupted
And instead of hugging the couch
I was gripping a brand new .45 …

The thing about shooting a hand cannon
Is once all is said and through
Not much else can bother you

No stress today.
Good interruption.

Propaganda #391

It's all a fucking joke.

It's about penis envy and power.

We are the unfortunate ones

That funded our own end,

Even when the struggle

Didn't have much to do with us.

Utopian Tuesday

If I'm doomed
To lose my mind
To begin with,
Then what's the issue
Having fun with it
While I have it?

A little bit of acid
Only ever caused
A little bit of mischief
And a few questions
Aimed at the right
People's choices.

If you can't learn
To love, then maybe
Ecstasy isn't such

A bad idea; Love yourself

Enough to love the

Freedom of others.

Detroit Red

Being told thinking is dangerous

By a man who bears authority

Is from the same playbook

That tells us order is needed.

No more death to the rebels.

No more death to the free thinkers.

Labeling everything but yourself

Is the 21st century's slavery.

What happens when both

The ballot and the bullet are outdated?

We should be evolved enough

To not need a debate or filibuster.

Thank you, Brother Malcolm...

Because you made me feel

Justified when I took my freedom

And forgot all about race.

Singing *"You Can't Stop Us Now,"*
You can't stop us now.

Propaganda #520

I've been told

Too many times

That I think too deep

Into things

By people too scared

To do better,

Be bigger.

Sun Rays

Sycophant, sycophant.
Aren't I by definition
Stuck in your inhibitions?

Wake up from the nightmare.
Wake up from the nightmare,
There's a butterfly on the windowsill…

Can't you hear it flapping?
Can't you hear the sun rays
Knocking on the glass?

Wake up from the nightmare.
Wake up from the nightmare,
There's a world outside the windowsill…

Floating Coconuts Part 4

There was a day
You wore a cute
Vest to school.
I remember thinking
It looked comfortable.

I wanted to hold
Your hand so bad
And got butterflies
At the dance
When I got close.

Now, with a sunset
Cascading through palm prongs,
A hammock, and iguanas
Wearing cute umbrellas;
Floating coconuts are
COMFORTABLE.

Propaganda #771

If they can't

Treat you

The way that

You treat you,

And vice versa,

It's time to let go.

Backyard Fractals

Sit down on my slab
And let me drain a bong.
Heat up the banger
And slam a 0.1 to the face.
Hold it in for a second
Until it takes you away.

There was a 1 second
First wave fractal
And a 1 second
Second wave multiplication.
1 second later was blast off
And I purged until I couldn't.

Two palm trees, a fence,
Coconuts, and the slab
Were memories from before
Being stuck in limbo.
How long was I there?

Was I just an experiment?
I'm dying, he overdosed me.

My brain is broken.
The grass's eyes stretched
For what seemed miles
With clear skies.
Geometric mountains on either side
Anytime I could look up.

Waves crash in and out.
So, I sat in them.
This it, this is how my life
Is going to be now.
I wanted off the roller coaster
But even if it was possible,
Would I really jump off?

Another deep breath
Brought me to peace
As I glided back home.
I was cold and warm,

Sound and silence.

The palm trees and coconuts

Regained their shape,

Slowly the fractals faded.

Almost immediately

I wanted to go back.

Things just made sense here.

I had to shower it away

And still more lingered.

So, I lounged most the day

Trying to piece reality

Back together.

Perception is key

Like most things in the universe,

Without it we find ourselves

As lost as the goldfish…

And maybe in another reality,

We are.

And maybe this is

That reality.

Texts Goodnight

She said in a Brazilian accent,

"I have a really stupid smile on my face now...

So, maybe I'm not the only one with

Magical voodoo powers..."

"Well I'm not the one who put

All these *borboletas* in my stomach"

Propaganda #022

One thing is certain:

You can't have a heart

In South Florida.

Past Shadows Linger

You don't
Have to worry...
You don't
Have to run.

Just stay a second to see
That they're all artificial sweetener
Pretending to be your sugar
In neon packets;
Held together
In caddies of conformity.
A silhouette of your shape
At a distance that distorts
As it gets closer and clearer.
Shapeshifters born to mimic
The angels in order
To infiltrate
The heaven
In my heart.

You don't
Have to worry...
You don't
Have to run.

I'll always
Love you.

Bullies

But, fear me.

I am the *Hibakusha*

Of when capitalism

Exploded.

And, fuck you.

It'd all be fine

If they left civilians

Alone.

No more division allowed

If we want to evolve.

No more human experiments

If it doesn't prolong.

But, fear me.

I am the Koreans

From when biology

Exploded.

And, fuck you.

It'd all be fine
If they left civilians
Alone.

Desecrated at birth
And much but nothing
Has changed.
Desecrate me now
Desecrate me forever.

Propaganda #382

There's nothing
More comfortable
Than doing drugs
With the kids you used to
In high school
13 years ago.

Boom, Gone

I have avocado'd hands
Turning brown from lack of humanity.

The idea of her
Was a great idea.

Paper doesn't always
Beat rock.

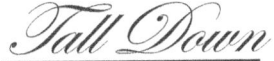

When the last of the weed

Burns out

And the LSD stash is dry,

And man learns

The language of his enemy.

Propaganda #242

If you call yourself an artist

And you don't get fucked up,

Then it's just craft hour

At the senior center,

You amateurs.

Timothy Leary once wrote

Of a long line of commuter cars

Of intellectual robots...

But how can one be an intellectual

And still be caught in those

Autonomous robotics

And waste such a large chunk

Of your brain, life,

And time alike?

Outbreak Day 115

I heard someone say we should
Feed them all to the nuns
And I wasn't sure who the food was.
Gross depictions of humanity
Are strafing from left to right,
Kids crying in the distance,
Coroners with a waiting list.

Too much order, too much order.
All we ever needed was a little
Chaos to balance the ordained
With the free and uncertain.
Only miscreants like us will
Prevail through these times
With grace and ease and
Exit on the other end stronger.

Tiddlywinks

Our first kiss was while

Trespassing on a stage

In a closed amphitheater.

I was looking for

The last job I was

Ever going to have.

Will you shut your mouth?

You're an amazing person.

You just don't have any milkshakes.

You want: 4 tacos

A milkshake

2 slices of pizza

And garlic rolls...

Oh my god, are you pregnant?

Will you shut your mouth?

You're an amazing person,

We just can't have any babies.

Our last kiss was
Beside your car before
You left last week.
I was hoping
It wasn't going
To be final.

Will you shut your mouth?
You're an amazing person.
I just don't ever
Want to see you again.

Woman Sitting at the Bus Stop with Son

She looked haggard in
A T-shirt from the
80s. Horizontal
White and blue stripes and
Whitewashed jeans. Her hair
Had missed a few ap-
pointments and she looked
As tired as she
Looked rushed at 2 in
The morning. Probab-
ly why she looked
Like she just yelled at
Her sad little boy.

The little boy stared in-
to limbo waiting
For the bus to bring

Him to bed. Little
Green corduroys with
A Spiderman T-
Shirt tucked in. He let
One of his arms slip
Off his knee; a move-
ment he had even
Less energy af-
ter. And despite be-
ing so tired, he
Looked like he knew he
Was a huge burden.

I rested my head
To forget the world.
A long day of ur-
ban hiking in heat
Jim Morrison would
Hide from. This bus must
Have been a differ-
ent line and I would
Not ever see them

Again. But would I
Ever forget? No.

We are all just wait-
ing for something to
Bring us all the way home.
I was that sad boy.

Propaganda #997

You keep shooting

For the stars

And you're going to

Need an eye patch.

If I Could Tell You

We've been sitting
In our own spoilage.
I apologize for what I said
When I ran out of coke
And for the freak out
When I was out of weed.

Bottling Time

I kissed you in all the right places
It's so good, I can tell when I taste it.
My eyes widen like your thighs
When you let me into paradise.

The memory of ten beautiful days
Can be blemished by a single spot of rain.
Like a shadow out of darkness

I turn them all into bad, bad girls
In a dark room with random men

Just for fun.

Propaganda #329

It's a crazy world outside.

Don't answer the door

After dark

Without a gun

In your waistband.

Kobe Bryant just died

In a helicopter crash

And there are crackheads

Trying to sell pussy

Next to my mailbox.

The smart move isn't

Walking up my driveway

Or telling me

You live next door.

Fuck you think this is

Around here?

Compass to the Heart

Turn your head to the left
And lock the door.
No ghosts nor demons,
No gods and no priests
Live here anymore.

Turn your mind to the right
And open the window.
There's nothing to fear,
No life to stand for
That you won't swallow.

Jump up one time
And where does that leave
All of the rest of us?
Long live the ebb and flow
Of the contagious disease.

Lay down and roll around

Until the fire inside
Dies in your arms.
Take up the emulsified soil;
Leave this place petrified.

Stand up to the open view
And take in a cigarette.
If it wasn't strong enough
Before you hit the ground,
Practice more etiquette.

And once you go to sleep,
Don't forget those you forgot.
And once you wake up,
Forget them once more;
To hell with the maggots.

There is a whole lake
In Leopold County.
What a perfect place
To hold the fuckin' trial
Once you pay off the bounty.

Retire here much more

Than you ever did at home.

There is more in the ashes

And more in the smoke

Than the whole phoenix that rose.

Delray Beach

Today I watched a beetle

Chase a centipede.

A guy getting crack

And a guy with a quota to meet.

A dog that's lost

And a cat with three feet.

I was listening to an old drunk,

Singing *"A Change Gon' Come,"*

In the middle of the street

That nothing will ever change from.

The night in the hood goes quiet.

Everything but crickets

And family problems

Know better than to make a snippet.

Snippets lead to gunshots,

Despite the public image.

Propaganda #722

Birds and flies are

The first living things

To habit an area destroyed,

Even before rats.

Hostess

She was a fiery dragon lady;
Mira has got machine guns
In her eyes.
Staring straight ahead
Like her day of reckoning
Is right behind her.

Too bad they were
Short-barreled without aim.
That's how one ends up
Trapped and running
Low on ammo.
But what is having a husband
Without having a boytoy
On the side?

Under My Arm

No one poem could ever

Do you justice, Beast;

No one song could ever encapsulate.

On plywood islands in pig shit paradise

With 3 feet of chain, who could've imagined

Such a beautiful Beast would grow.

I remember telling you that roast beef sub

Would change your life, did I lie?

They put you in the car and

You curled up under my arm.

How'd you know I'd give you something better?

Was it that bad there?

The scar above your eye and the way

You flinch at a raised hand screams, "YES!"

Yes, it was terror and torture, malnutrition and neglect.

I bet they never noticed how

You sleep on one of your paws

And I wish they saw the way you hid your face

Under my arm; telling me you didn't care where

I took you as long as it was

With me and not back there.

And that's why we call them

Tripping and turn them into PETA

Or send them a bag of gummy dicks.

But no more.

No more hunger pains or cold nights.

No more needing love

Because you're loved until eternity ends.

You helped me through suicides and overdoses,

Car crashes and abandonment. We made heartbreak

And homelessness our bitch that bowed.

I bet they never heard you sigh in boredom

Once you know there is nothing more to protect,

Or the look of fear from doing the wrong thing.

The touchstone fact you still want

to please and trust us humans

Is a testament to what a pure soul you truly are.

I don't think I would be alive today without you.

And as you snore under my arm,

I'm writing this,

Planning our next trip outside

For howling at the moon.

Propaganda #213

Don't fear,

For it is a strange

New world outside.

But the sun rays

Never left us lonely

It's just much more

Destructive.

Be the Spark

Like cloves in the garbage,
I am the escape.
Just put me on your tongue
And wait.

It says to repeat twice a day
On the back of the bottle
But I'd up the dosage double;
Full throttle.

Last Floating Coconuts

"Ha!"

"They just get drunk and high"

"How you doin' young man"

"Somebody PLEASE help me"

"Ah, *Lawddd* help 'em!"

"AAAHHH!"

"Alright, young man. How you?"

"Looks like that palm
Has the last floating coconuts."

"Whewwwwwwww!"

Propaganda #174

Nothing is sadder
Than the man
Who moves across country
And still makes
The same mistakes
As in his hometown.

Insanity and death
Are never far apart.
Especially in a land
Of strange ways
And faces.

Biker Gang Graffiti

James Dean and rebels without causes
And an afterglow from mushrooms and ecstasy.
Lethargic teeth and Sand Buffalos
Made the Beast and I dread
The charge into sand dunes ahead.

Raleigh brought his own prescription,
Funny, it was the same as ours.
Fuck it if we run low tomorrow.
We can always double the dose tonight,
Good despicables do it despite.

Good friends they were to resist;
Even porn stars couldn't pull us away
From cigarette smoke and cheap whiskey.
So, on to a biker bar it was
Of course, with drinks and on drugs.

"If your phone is out, keep it flat on the bar,"

Was just one of the many rules.

What a funny concept that was,

Outlaws to society following rules.

I guess order is just another one of their tools.

But who cares when they pour Jack like that?

They kept us included with the weed

And their coke was definitely necessary.

"Just go out back, into the bathroom.

We left you a line right next to the vacuum."

Blacking out is easy in an all-black room.

Nothing can spin if can't see it move,

And waking up on the wrong side of the bed

Just means I had a good time last night

And a killer hangover to fight.

Works in 30 and I'm completely dressed,

But I'm not sure I can stand up from the couch.

Maybe I'll make a decision in 15.

Maybe I won't and call it a day.

After all, fuck that job anyways.

Peace.

Linear

People in small towns

Love small jokes

To make them go

Der-der-derrr.

Some of my most beloved things

About Christmas in South Florida

Are all of the lights and none of the snow

Or dealing with their low-tensibility

Lives ever again.

String-thin,

Linear bastards.

Propaganda #265

Staring at the ocean

Triggers thoughts

The world is behind you

All your problems

Are behind you

You are the last

Person in your way

Negativity spawns

Where negativity

Lies

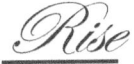 Rise

Don't worry your pretty mind

With words wrote years ago

When my face was less scruffy.

Toast a glass full of Coyote Blood

And relax knowing it won't take long to set in.

After its over, there isn't a thing to do but resurrect

The lost flame of anarchism and drench

Your following in distilled bullocks.

As long as you add some MSG

To the distilling process and malt only premium

GMO bullock seeds, you'll create the demand

Where there's plenty supply.

Monster

When you're sad
Is when you're most cute
And I'm addicted to you.

But that's the thing
About addiction;
It doesn't come without

The abuse.
Let me be that
Monster for you.

Propaganda # 663

Don't listen to the propaganda
If you want to keep living your life
The way it is; for knowledge is
The biggest catalyst for change.

If You Feel Like I Do

Enjoy the shrooms…

And don't forget

To write

icon303

On the moon

While you're there.

Why So Mad, Alice?

Sometimes I find it
Hard to write like me
When I'm different
Than I was last year,
Month, day, hour.

And even though
4 years ago, I was
Sitting on my couch
High on acid, today
I'm doing much of the same.

Maybe, take a walk
And see what the hood
Has to offer? The comical snips
From the corner alcoholics
Will surely give me some
Insight into their mindset.
Maybe one will set himself up

For a juggs and I can get myself
A soda and a pack of smokes.
They'd never expect it from me,
But I'm never that lucky.

The streetlamps were twined
With rope lights that
Doubled themselves into
A four-dimensional hologram
That was one of the most
Beautiful sights I've ever seen.
Every streetlamp. Every. One.
How could I explain it
To someone who has
Never seen it before?

Maybe mention a couple of ways
That it makes you feel.
Or, maybe, some of the things you see.
But would they really get it?
Would it really make sense?
Or would they have to wait until

Watching a lizard eat an ant

Showed you how much

You don't matter?

More of the latter.

Drugs never hurt the right people.

So, excuse me, good sir,

But, fuck your opinion.

Propaganda #323

Television has morphed

Into a form of

Social media in itself.

Becoming moderators and monitors,

Judges and commentators,

Analysts, and experts,

To our social media platforms.

One that we all,

Deep down, hope to make it on.

One could argue,

The biggest form of social media.

With things like movies

And shows being

The only accepted forms

Of *censored* expression.

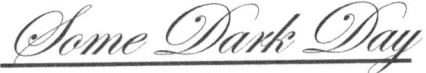

I'm not much of a talker.
Let me curl up in a dark cave
Until the rain stops.

I'm not much for trust.
No offense, but I've learned:
Born, live, die alone.

Maybe someone will find me.
I just hope I don't smell;
In due time.

Conceptualize

Imagine if Arthur Miller
Knew the truth
That we still don't.

Do you think he would
Be as disappointed
As we are in the
Bipartisan voting system
Or the secrets of the universe?
Would he be upset none of us
Know about Vortex Mathematics
Or higher frequencies?
"Imagine if we knew the truth,"
He said.

In knowledge we failed
And compassion we're bust.
Now, in *God* we rust.

Propaganda #811

Snowbirds

Are the worst type of human.

Above Nazis,

Racists, and communists,

Because they're all

The above combined.

The only thing comparable

Are old, born-rich, Jewish widows.

Last Hammock in the Outer Rim

I think I found a way out of here.

There's a bag of potato chips

At a bus stop and a young lady

Hoping to retire on the moon;

Much like my desires to lounge

In a hammock under the palms

Smoking weed all day.

I left it all behind for this here.

This right here is pandora unboxed;

Sun rays on my face, a cool breeze

To carry away the stress I blew.

A cool breeze of the submission

And disowning of my former life.

A freeing wind that brought about

A deep appreciation for lizards

And sand and sun and rebirth.

Fuck retribution and past dues.

Fuck saying goodbye to the things

You hold most dear in inhabitance.

Pick up the bag of chips and
Change your whole perspective.
Maybe one day you can retire
On the moon beside the young lady;
Exploring craters and telling stories
Of the dark side and a time before.
It's weightless in those spacesuits,
As coincidental as it may be to those
Inside the coloring lines provided.

The whole god damn paper is slag
And the publisher pissed off
The printing company after the
Ink was dry on the contracts.
Might as well roll it up and
Set the end on fire before you
Breathe in the bullshit, *mèsi*.

Kitty Kitty Kitty

I thought of you yesterday,

Speaking of a field full of nightshade.

I found some seeds and I don't know

If they're quite legal, you see?

But I thought of you, get it?

You'll go down as being

One of the most beautiful poems

That I was too scared to write.

Me and my unruly beard hairs

Were up at like 4AM to make a sandwich

And write poetry in the dark

With one eye open.

What is it called when

Solitude changes into

Its final winter phase?

A mobster can't predict

His own cancer.

Just know when I say I love you

That there is no monetary value
Or ulterior motives.

I'd give anything to see
You waiting for me
On your stairs with
All your cats.
I regret not kissing you
The minute I had the chance.
And, I'm sorry for everything
You've had to go through
Because I didn't.

Propaganda #212

Watch the scene after the credits

In Justice League 2017

And see my name

On a floating billboard.

It's a sign.

Trips to the Moon 2

I shed a tear for the
Poor bastards that are blind.
To go through life
Without the beauty.

Everyone else is overdosing.

Bartender to pay bills;
Poet, artist, writer to pay my soul.
When it comes down to it,
I am Physically less important than
What I have to say.

Maybe I act like
I'm 95 because
I'm destined to die at 50.
The only thing that matters
Is that you tap the brake lights
3 times if you see a cop ahead.

Who would hear me even if my lungs
Weren't black trash bags by now?
I'm one of those warriors assumed
From stars, sun, and the moon.

Another coconut sunset and that girl
That passed me making me feel pretty.
Where is the fashion in a
Badge no one can have?

My friends are all dead rebels
Because there is no such thing
As order in the real world.
It's all just chaos.
That is perfection, that is freedom.

But what happens
When I become
Just a normal person
To you?

Dog Day

The Beast is kicking her feet

While she's probably dreaming

Of the last time she ate a gram of coke;

Her face snug with a squeaky bottle of Jameson.

Propaganda #124

I said it before:

The right ones will laugh,

The right ones will cry.

But I left out that

The right ones will also

Never give a fuck.

Instance of Instants

For an instant we forget
The need for humanity
In times like such ahead
That in an instant, we lose
Our moral compass
And compassion for those
Around us also in darkness

For an instant it seemed
Hope was gone
And in an instant, we lost it
All together in unison.

For an instant it sang
Like help was a hand reach
Away when you needed it
That in an instant, it felt
Like there was no help
Miles in either direction

To hear your cries.

For an instant it seemed
Love was gone
And in an instant, we lost it
All together in unison.

For an instant it felt safer
Than what was going
On around us recently
That in an instant, we folded
What we used to know
Into a naively wrapped square.

For an instant it seemed
Freedom was gone
And in an instant, we lost it
All together in unison.

Fox Lady Supreme

We were on the right path,

30 rack under each arm.

One of us skated ahead,

But the three of us were totally behind.

The alleyway was overgrown

With pines and vines and

A forgotten cobblestone barrier.

So overgrown that the next few houses

Were as much as a surprise as

The little middle-aged woman asking

Us about foxes. Foxes, you say?

Well, we only see you and

The rest of the evening

Us pondering if you're crazy.

Maybe just a little eccentric

In your approach, but maybe just

Trying to meet someone new.

We took that route the next few times

But never saw you or

Any of those shrewd foxes.

Propaganda #093

Drugs are often irrationally

Stigmatized

By people

Who have never

Done them

Properly.

Epoxy

Only delineated swirls
Distract me from
The fact I can still see
Right through.

Yet I'm still
The one who knows
What the barrel of his
Gun tastes like.

Propaganda #551

Don't let the problems of today

Sully your total self-worth

Tomorrow.

Never Let Go

Yugo looked at the Beast

And asked,

"Can't you just live

As long as me, Fatty?"

Like a worry-stone,

Yugo placed all my sorrows

On the Beast's stable shoulders;

Rubbing them into

Her coat and extra skin.

"Tell me why I can't go with you."

Outbreak day 331

We jammed out the house
With "*Castles Made of Sand*"
By The Jimi Hendrix Experience
And shooting guns at coconuts
In the back yard. What better?
Our castle was made of sand
And some of us saw it coming.

Rations are as scarce as
The stars staring back at us;
Useless to help and gasping
While watching us consume
Ourselves from within.
Just like the castles.

The good, yet scary thing is:
The internet is still on...
But that bares the question of
Who the fuck is running

This rigmarole and what,
Oh, what, are we going to do
When the 1s and 0s stop answering?

We'll certainly implode
Without a screen
That works in our face.

Good thing is:
There is plenty of ammunition.
Time to take what you want.

Propaganda #767

Somethings aren't worth

Their own weight in anxiety.

If all you'll ever need

Is in your small hometown,

Then there's no point

In talking to me in Florida.

Because, right now it's raining coconuts

And I'm enthralled with the landscape.

It brings an air of chaos

To break up the monotony.

Everything in life has a curve;

A rise and a fall

To a plateau of

Ordinary.

See

You

Assholes

On

The

Other

Side.

I'll

Be

The

One

Smoking

Weed

Next

To

The

No

Smoking

Sign

-icon303

www.ingramcontent.com/pod-product-compliance
Lightning Source LLC
Chambersburg PA
CBHW070540220526
45467CB00003B/1011

* 9 7 9 8 7 1 3 8 0 3 1 5 5 *